STRING BASS

PATRIOTIC FAVORITES

Solos and String Orchestra Arrangements
Correlated with Essential Elements String Method

Arranged by
JOHN MOSS

Welcome to Essential Elements Patriotic Favorites! There are two versions of each selection in this versatile book. The SOLO version appears in the beginning of your book. The STRING ORCHESTRA arrangements of each song follows. The supplemental CD recording or string orchestra PIANO PART may be used as an accompaniment for solo performance. Use these recordings when playing solos for friends and family.

Solo Page	String Arr. Page	Title	Correlated with Essential Elements
2	13	God Bless America	Book 2, page 30
3	14	Yankee Doodle	Book 1, page 34
4	15	The Caissons Go Rolling Along/ Anchors Aweigh	Book 2, page 30
5	16	My Country, 'Tis Of Thee (America)/ America, The Beautiful	Book 2, page 30
6	17	The Patriot	Book 2, page 43
7	18	Marine's Hymn	Book 1, page 34
8	19	Stars And Stripes Forever	Book 2, page 43
9	20	Battle Hymn Of The Republic	Book 2, page 43
10	21	This Is My Country	Book 2, page 43
11	22	The Star Spangled Banner	Book 2, page 30
12	23	Hymn To The Fallen	Book 2, page 43

ISBN 978-0-634-05282-8

7777 W. BLUEMOUND RD. P.O. BOX 13819 MILWAUKEE, WI 53213

For all works contained herein:
Unauthorized copying, arranging, adapting, recording, or
public performance is an infringement of copyright.
Infringers are liable under the law.

Visit Hal Leonard Online at
www.halleonard.com

GOD BLESS AMERICA

STRING BASS
Solo

Words and Music by
IRVING BERLIN
Arranged by JOHN MOSS

YANKEE DOODLE

STRING BASS
Solo

Traditional
Arranged by JOHN MOSS

MY COUNTRY, 'TIS OF THEE (AMERICA)/ AMERICA, THE BEAUTIFUL

STRING BASS
Solo

Arranged by JOHN MOSS

MY COUNTRY, 'TIS OF THEE (AMERICA)
Words by SAMUEL FRANCIS SMITH
Music from THESAURUS MUSICUS
Copyright © 2003 by HAL LEONARD CORPORATION
International Copyright Secured   All Rights Reserved

AMERICA, THE BEAUTIFUL
Words by KATHERINE LEE BATES
Music by SAMUEL A. WARD
Copyright © 2003 by HAL LEONARD CORPORATION
International Copyright Secured   All Rights Reserved

MARINE'S HYMN

STRING BASS
Solo

Words by HENRY C. DAVIS
Melody based on a theme by
JACQUES OFFENBACH
Arranged by JOHN MOSS

STARS AND STRIPES FOREVER

STRING BASS
Solo

By JOHN PHILIP SOUSA
Arranged by JOHN MOSS

BATTLE HYMN OF THE REPUBLIC

STRING BASS
Solo

Words by JULIA WARD HOWE
Music by WILLIAM STEFFE
Arranged by JOHN MOSS

THIS IS MY COUNTRY

STRING BASS
Solo

Words by DON RAYE
Music by AL JACOBS
Arranged by JOHN MOSS

HYMN TO THE FALLEN

From the Paramount and DreamWorks Motion Picture SAVING PRIVATE RYAN

STRING BASS
Solo

JOHN WILLIAMS
Arranged by JOHN MOSS

YANKEE DOODLE

STRING BASS
String Orchestra Arrangement

Traditional
Arranged by JOHN MOSS

THE CAISSONS GO ROLLING ALONG / ANCHORS AWEIGH

String Bass
String Orchestra Arrangement

Arranged by JOHN MOSS

THE CAISSONS GO ROLLING ALONG
Words and Music by EDMUND L. GRUBER
Copyright © 2003 by HAL LEONARD CORPORATION
International Copyright Secured   All Rights Reserved

ANCHORS AWEIGH
Words by ALFRED HART MILES and ROYAL LOVELL
Music by CHARLES A. ZIMMERMAN
Additional Lyric by GEORGE D. LOTTMAN
Copyright © 2003 by HAL LEONARD CORPORATION
International Copyright Secured   All Rights Reserved

MARINE'S HYMN

STRING BASS
String Orchestra Arrangement

Words by HENRY C. DAVIS
Melody based on a theme by
JACQUES OFFENBACH
Arranged by JOHN MOSS

Stars and Stripes Forever

STRING BASS
String Orchestra Arrangement

By JOHN PHILIP SOUSA
Arranged by JOHN MOSS

BATTLE HYMN OF THE REPUBLIC

STRING BASS
String Orchestra Arrangement

Words by JULIA WARD HOWE
Music by WILLIAM STEFFE
Arranged by JOHN MOSS

Copyright © 2003 by HAL LEONARD CORPORATION
International Copyright Secured   All Rights Reserved

THIS IS MY COUNTRY

STRING BASS
String Orchestra Arrangement

Words by DON RAYE
Music by AL JACOBS
Arranged by JOHN MOSS

© 1940 SHAWNEE PRESS, INC.
© Renewed SHAWNEE PRESS, INC. and WAROCK CORP.
This arrangement © 2003 SHAWNEE PRESS, INC. and WAROCK CORP.
All Rights Reserved

THE STAR SPANGLED BANNER

STRING BASS
String Orchestra Arrangement

Words by FRANCIS SCOTT KEY
Music by JOHN STAFFORD SMITH
Arranged by JOHN MOSS

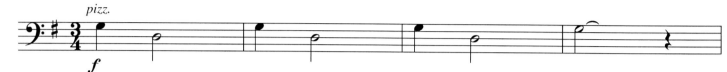

Copyright © 2003 by HAL LEONARD CORPORATION
International Copyright Secured   All Rights Reserved

00868067